THE LIVING GOSPEL

Daily Devotions for Advent 2018

THE LIVING GOSPEL

Daily Devotions for Advent 2018

Greg Kandra

Ave Maria Press AVE Notre Dame, Indiana

Founded in 1865, Ave Maria Press is a ministry of the United States Province of Holy Cross.

www.avemariapress.com

Paperback: ISBN-13 978-1-59471-843-4

E-book: ISBN-13 978-1-59471-844-1

Cover image "Approaching Bethlehem" © 2012 by Jeni Butler, artworkbyjeni.wix.com/art.

Cover and text design by John R. Carson.

Printed and bound in the United States of America.

Introduction

I live not far from a synagogue in Queens, New York, that has a plaque hanging on an outside wall, dedicated to Helen Keller. The legendary blind and deaf writer once lived in a house that stood on that spot. Sometimes I walk past and wonder whether the neighborhood has changed much since her day. For just a moment, I close my eyes and imagine, what she felt, what she sensed, and what she feared.

It must have been terrifying. She couldn't hear the cars, or the children on bicycles, or the stirring of the leaves in the wind. Did she know if someone was approaching her? She would hear no footfalls, no voices. Would she even know if it was daylight?

Little wonder, then, that Helen Keller once famously summed up our existence with this simple proclamation: "Life is either a daring adventure, or nothing." In her universe, every moment was an adventure. It had to be. Otherwise she would have remained forever a prisoner of her imperfect senses.

Well, we get some idea of the daring that life involves as we begin the season of Advent. Whether we realize it or not, we're embarking on an adventure of our own. After all, the name of this season shares the same root as "adventure"—from the Latin *adventus*, meaning arrival. The arrival we await, of course, is that of the Messiah—God incarnate, Jesus. And what an adventure that waiting will be!

It's always good to have company when you're doing something adventurous, and so it is my hope that these brief reflections will serve as a companion for the journey toward Christmas—offering a fresh way of thinking about and experiencing this holy time. Each day is structured very simply, to allow a busy Christian to find just a few minutes every day to reflect on the world around us—to be still and be with God.

The waiting can be a challenge. Now, in early December, the nights grow longer and the weather turns colder. We are as far as we can ever be from the sun, but we know in our bones and in our hearts that this darkness will not last. So we wait it out. We light candles. We decorate trees. But there is so much to do, too! As the nights lengthen and the light dims, we shop, we wrap, we spend time in long lines at the post office and bear gifts for one another and attend parties where we drink too much eggnog and make too many promises we never manage to keep.

And we sing. *O come, o come Emmanuel.* When will we be ransomed? When will we find rest? When will our Rescuer arrive?

At the start of Advent, as we begin this adventure, we are striking out, stepping boldly into the dark. But we are not alone. We will encounter many other travelers along the way. A young girl will run to her cousin to announce a miracle. Later, she and her husband will travel toward a stable. Wise men will set out to follow a star. We may find ourselves disoriented at the turn the road takes.

But we remember what Helen Keller wrote: "Life is either a daring adventure, or nothing." And we feel certain we are heading in the right direction. We take heart, and take hope. We know there will again be light. But for now, we wait.

Advent is a time of perpetual anticipation. Dorothy Day once compared this season of expectation to pregnancy: it is like a mother waiting to give birth. She was a mother, and she understood that analogy well.

But I keep going back to her contemporary, Helen Keller, who once wrote something that makes me wonder if Dorothy Day had it backward. Keller wrote, in a very different context: "Everything has its wonders, even darkness and silence." Could it be that the power of this season lies not in waiting to give birth, but in waiting to be born? Perhaps we are the ones in the womb, in darkness and silence, waiting, in every sense, to be delivered. Either way, I think, this moment in time—this waiting, this anticipation, this expectancy, this Advent— is a daring adventure.

And it is not nothing—in fact, it is *everything*. Let's get started.

SUNDAY, DECEMBER 2
FIRST WEEK OF ADVENT

BEGIN

"Be still, and know that I am God."

PRAY

Your ways, O Lord, make known to me;
teach me your paths,
Guide me in your truth and teach me,
for you are God my savior,
and for you I wait all the day.

~Psalm 25:4–5

LISTEN

Read Luke 21:25–28, 34–26.

"Be vigilant at all times."

~Luke 21:36

What Are You Waiting For?

What are *you* waiting for right now?

Most people would say: I'm waiting for Christmas, the birth of Jesus! I'm waiting for parties and presents, cards and carols. But the gospel reading that begins our Advent season suggests something else. We are waiting for an event that transcends the tinsel and the tree—it even transcends time.

What we are waiting for, really, is the *end* of time.

We are waiting for Christ to come, yes—to come not as a baby in a manger, but as a King-on-earth. This means that Advent isn't simply a time for buying and baking, but for searching our hearts and making choices. The word "advent" calls attention to the event described in today's gospel reading. The Latin word *adventus* is often a translation of the Greek *parousia*, which refers to Christ's second coming. As we pray at every Mass: "We wait in joyful hope for the coming of our savior, Jesus Christ."

Advent doesn't merely commemorate what was but anticipates what will be. And it calls *us* to *be*. To be watchful. To be ready.

"Be vigilant at all times," Jesus told his followers. Don't let your heart become drowsy from the anxieties of life. In our own time, that isn't easy. We are constantly distracted. We have the nightly news, C-SPAN, and social media blaring grim tidings. Which brings us back to the great questions of Advent: What are you waiting for? What are *we all* waiting for?

As we will hear so often this season, "O come Emmanuel, and ransom captive Israel." We are a world in chains. Advent reminds us the chains will be broken. In the darkest of days, we will soon know light. Candle by candle, flame by flame, Advent reminds us: there is hope!

ACT

This day, I will think of the words of the great hymn of this season, pleading for the world to be ransomed and contemplate what chains are holding me. From what do I want to be freed? I will pray that God free me.

PRAY

O come, o come, Emmanuel! God, be with me! Free me from what holds us captive. Amen.

Monday, December 3
First Week of Advent

BEGIN

"Be still, and know that I am God."

PRAY

Because of my relatives and friends
I will say, "Peace be within you!"
Because of the house of the LORD, our God,
I will pray for your good.

~Psalm 122:8–9

LISTEN

Read Matthew 8:5–11.

"Lord, I am not worthy to have you enter under
my roof; only say the word and my servant will be
healed."

~Matthew 8:8

God with Us

Think about it: the centurion saw Jesus and believed in
him through the filter of his own experience. He was a
Roman soldier, after all, not a Jew. Yet he understood
this Jewish carpenter and teacher as someone a lot like
himself: a figure of authority who could command men
to be healed, the way he himself could command them to
march or go into battle. He recognized Jesus as someone
who got things done.

In some ways, this anonymous centurion becomes
for us today the perfect herald of Advent—reminding
us that God comes to us in the Incarnation in a form all

of us can understand. He comes into our world as we all do, as a helpless infant.

With people such as the centurion and the servant, this gospel passage also forces us to ask if we are doing enough to recognize Christ in others. Do we look for him in those around us? Do we seek him in those who are different from us? Do we relate to Christ in a human and personal way? Or do we see him as distant and detached? Are we, in fact, distant and detached from him?

These weeks of Advent are an opportunity to grow in our awareness of God's presence in our lives as we see his presence in others around us. The name "Emmanuel" means "God with us." Do we see how God is with us in those we love, those we know, those we pass on the street? How often do I look for God in others? Have I forgotten that we are all made in his image? What do I see—*whom* do I see—when I pass someone hungry, alone, or hurting?

ACT

Today I will seek the presence of God in the people I meet and open myself to the grace they bring. I will show kindness and mercy to those in need, no matter how great or small, and I will thank the Lord for those who challenge me, bring me joy, or show me how to love.

PRAY

O come, o come, Emmanuel! God, be with me as I seek your face. Amen.

TUESDAY, DECEMBER 4
FIRST WEEK OF ADVENT

BEGIN

"Be still, and know that I am God."

PRAY

He shall rescue the poor when he cries out,
and the afflicted when he has no one to help him.

~Psalm 72:12

LISTEN

Read Luke 10:21–24.

"I give you praise, Father, Lord of heaven and earth,
for although you have hidden these things
from the wise and the learned
you have revealed them to the childlike."

~Luke 10:21

Seeking Awe

I remember the year my mother took me to see Santa at the shopping center when I was five. I climbed onto his lap, and he listened to what I wanted for Christmas—a two-wheel Schwinn bicycle—and then replied, "I'll do what I can. But you have to do one thing first." I looked up, breathless, and swallowed hard. He continued. "You have to promise me you'll stop sucking your thumb."

Busted!

I was stunned. He knew I sucked my thumb?! Wow. I vowed never to do it again. I climbed off his lap and went back to my mother, amazed at what the guy in the white beard and red velvet suit had known about me.

According to my parents, I never sucked my thumb after that, ever.

As we get older, we tend to lose that sense of wonder. We grow jaded, cynical, and skeptical. Doubt creeps in.

But look around. These weeks, we'll see kids around us anticipating something magical. As we hear in the gospel: those who are childlike understand. They await Christmas morning with wonder.

But the wonder should go beyond the shopping mall sentiment of asking Santa for presents; our yearning in these days goes deeper. It is about our expectation for the greatest gift: God with us, Emmanuel.

It is about welcoming grace.

That Christmas long ago, I kept my end of the bargain, and so did Santa. I ended up getting the bike I wanted. But every year, I try to remember the enchantment of being five, a time when Advent carried inexplicable mystery, wonder, and hope. I was awed back then. Why shouldn't this season fill me with awe now?

ACT

It is too easy these days to grow cynical or jaded. My heart can grow hard. Advent is an opportunity to change that. I will work today to seek the best in others and in every situation to seek the wonder in the world around me, grateful for how God surprises me every day.

PRAY

O come, o come, Emmanuel! God, be with me! Teach me again to know wonder. Amen.

WEDNESDAY, DECEMBER 5
FIRST WEEK OF ADVENT

BEGIN

"Be still, and know that I am God."

PRAY

Even though I walk in the dark valley
I fear no evil; for you are at my side
With your rod and your staff
that give me courage.

~Psalm 21:4

LISTEN

Read Matthew 15:29–37.

They all ate and were satisfied.
They picked up the fragments left over—seven baskets full.

~Matthew 15:37

All People Matter

One of the most inspiring groups around is the Jesuit
Volunteer Corps (JVC): an international group of mostly
young people who work full time for justice and peace.
It's a remarkable organization that's been quietly doing
the work of the gospel for sixty years. They work for
and with people who are homeless or unemployed, refugees, people with AIDS, the elderly, street youth, abused
women and children, the mentally ill, and the developmentally disabled. More than 250 grassroots organizations across the world count on these volunteers.

A few years ago, the JVC sold T-shirts with a beautiful message on the front of each: "All people matter," it says. "No one is disposable." In so many ways, that is one of the key messages of this gospel reading. After Jesus performed the great miracle of multiplication, he saw to it that nothing went to waste—even the smallest fragments were collected and saved. Isn't that why Jesus came into the world? To see that no one is overlooked?

This gospel reminds us that the King we are awaiting cares for all and will neglect no one. Christ entered human history as the humblest and neediest of creatures. To many he was just a fragment—someone easily discarded, someone that nobody had room for at the inn in Bethlehem. He came to feed all who hunger, nourish all in need, and find all who are lost. Be assured and know this Advent hope: No one is disposable.

ACT

Today I will take one action to assist a person or group who is profoundly marginalized in my local community. I will choose from among direct service, financial support, and policy advocacy, and before day's end have a plan in place to help someone who feels neglected or forgotten—recalling that Jesus was once just such an outcast.

PRAY

O come, o come, Emmanuel! God, be with me as I work to set my eyes on those who live on the margins. Amen.

Thursday, December 6
First Week of Advent

BEGIN

"Be still, and know that I am God."

PRAY

Give thanks to the Lord, for he is good,
for his mercy endures forever.

~Psalm 118:1

LISTEN

Read Matthew 7:21, 24–27.

"Everyone who listens to these words of mine and
acts on them will be like a wise man who built his
house on rock."

~Matthew 7:24

Why It Matters

Several years ago, my wife's parents celebrated their
fiftieth wedding anniversary with a special Mass. They
invited a few dozen family and friends, and they asked
me to preach the homily. I chose for the gospel this particular reading, which I've always considered a good one
for weddings. Part of my homily that day went like this:

"You've reminded us that a marriage, like a house,
will survive change, and stand, only when it's made of
the right materials. And they're not the kind you find at
Home Depot. You've secured the walls with patience,
and tenderness, and prayer. You've installed a heating
system that is cooled by laughter. And you have made
sure that the roof is supported with love. Love for one

another. Love for your children. Love for God. You have built it all on a solid foundation—the rock of faith."

In marriage, as in so many things in life, it is easy to forget what truly matters. We get overwhelmed by responsibilities, headaches, pressures, problems, conflicts. It's the same in these weeks before Christmas, whether we're married or not. During this busy time of year, we can find ourselves swamped. There are gifts to buy, parties to plan, houses to decorate, credit cards to max out . . . the list can be endless. It is one reason we hear this refrain so often: "Jesus is the reason for the season."

Are we taking time during this frenetic four weeks to remember—*really* remember—the reason for it all?

While we enjoy the whirlwind of activity, let's build this season of grace on a solid foundation of prayer and faith—anticipating the great feast to come and celebrating why it matters.

ACT

Today I will carve out at least ten minutes to sit still and contemplate the reason for this season. I will choose one small act to show Advent hope to one other person this day.

PRAY

O come, o come, Emmanuel! God, be with me this day in the quiet stillness of my heart. Build in me a strong foundation. Amen.

Friday, December 7
First Week of Advent

BEGIN

"Be still, and know that I am God."

PRAY

The Lord is my light and my salvation.

~Psalm 27:1

LISTEN

Read Matthew 9:21, 27–31.

Then he touched their eyes and said,
"Let it be done for you according to your faith."
And their eyes were opened.

~Matthew 27:29–30

Do You Believe?

We hear it again and again this time of year: "I can't believe it's almost Christmas!"

Where does the time go? It seems like it gets shorter every year. We are still in the early days of Advent, but it doesn't seem there are enough days to get everything done. We can't believe it.

But this brief gospel takes us out of our seasonal frenzy and forces us to focus our hearts elsewhere. It brings us Jesus as he asks a defining, challenging question about belief: "Do you believe I can do this?"

Do *we* believe?

The beautiful lesson of this miracle is simple: believe and you will be given the gift of sight. Darkness will vanish. Your life will be filled with light. You will be astonished at the world that lies before you. Your eyes will be opened.

Just believe. It sounds so simple. But we know how hard faith, true faith, can be. We find ourselves easily discouraged, disappointed, and doubting. But the great feast we are approaching celebrates the wonder of believing the unbelievable—that God came into the world to dwell with us as one of us. We rejoice in what Christmas meant—and means.

This is a moment to banish doubt and to trust. It is a time to believe. Believe in possibility. Believe in God's overwhelming love—a love that can heal and bring light. Believe in sharing that love, that light with others. Believe that the coming of Jesus into the world changed everything and that it continues to change everything. That is the greatest miracle.

Do we believe?

ACT

I will strive this day to banish doubt and cynicism, and to believe in God's grace and goodness in the world. I will look for it in my life, in my family, and in my friends. And I will bear witness to my belief today in my words, my actions, my prayers, and my encounters with others.

PRAY

O come, o come, Emmanuel! God, be with me and strengthen my belief. Amen.

Saturday, December 8
Solemnity of the Immaculate Conception of the Blessed Virgin Mary

BEGIN

"Be still, and know that I am God."

PRAY

Sing to the LORD a new song,
for he has done wondrous deeds.

~Psalm 98:1

LISTEN

Read Luke 1:26–38.

"Nothing will be impossible with God."

~Luke 1:37

Recall the Wonder

A popular carol from this time of year rejoices in the "wonders of his love." The Feast of the Immaculate Conception underscores the extravagant love that brought joy to the world. And it places before us a humble peasant girl "full of grace," the great collaborator in God's plan for our salvation.

This day, in particular, we remember it is a salvation that began long before the first gospel was written. Rather, it is a salvation that in a real and tangible way began with the event we commemorate here and now: the Immaculate Conception of Mary.

This is where Mary's story begins—and, in a sense, our story, too. Here we begin to see more clearly the glorious chain of events that led to our salvation.

We must pay attention. We need to hold the wonder of his love close to our hearts and to keep recalling it—just like all the other great moments of our history, these moments define us and uplift us, and bear, somehow, the fingerprints of God.

Isn't it all a wonder? If Mary's story teaches us anything about our own lives, it is that our God is a God of surprises. He is the maker of miracles.

As we near the halfway point of Advent, during this season of anticipation and yearning, we pause to give thanks for the miracle of Mary—an immaculate sign of God's enduring love, a figure of steadfast hope, and the woman who reminds us again and again that in God's hands, truly, nothing is impossible.

ACT

Today I call to mind and give thanks for the wonder-filled moments of my life. I will pray to become more aware of the wonder of God's love and remember that he is the maker of miracles—nothing is impossible with God!

PRAY

O come, o come, Emmanuel! God, be with me and fill me with wonder. Amen.

SUNDAY, DECEMBER 9
SECOND WEEK OF ADVENT

BEGIN

"Be still, and know that I am God."

PRAY

The Lord has done great things for us; we are filled
with joy.

~Psalm 126:1–2

LISTEN

Read Luke 3:1–6.

John went throughout the whole region of the Jordan,
proclaiming a baptism of repentance for the forgive-
ness of sins.

~Luke 3:2–3

Make Way

When we think about these weeks before Christmas,
most of us probably don't think about operating heavy
machinery such as cranes, tractors, backhoes, and earth-
movers. But the fact is, there is work to be done. The
prophet Isaiah cries out to us in the scripture this week,
telling us to level the mountains, fill in the valleys, and
straighten the roads.

Prepare the way!

But he's talking about more than moving dirt. He's
talking about each of us moving our hearts, reorienting
ourselves to God. There is work to do before our Savior
arrives.

We are challenged to change everything around us,
to redraw the map of our lives. So let's ask ourselves:

What are the mountains we're living with? What are the barriers keeping others out—and keeping us in? Maybe it's the rocky hill of ambition. Or the flat wall of anger. Or the slippery slope of envy. What are the valleys we descend into? What are the winding, crooked roads we follow? The geography may be so much more complicated and challenging than we realize.

The voice in the desert, John the Baptist, calls out to each of us: look at your world! Survey the landscape. How can we regain our bearings?

Ask for the grace to clear the way—doing that will make it easier for God to enter in. Break out the shovels. Fire up the equipment. There is work to do!

ACT

What are the obstacles in my life that make it harder for God to find his way into my heart? What mountains are making it harder for love to enter? Mistrust? Selfishness? Pride? Today I will prayerfully work to clear them away, embracing the opportunity to respond with generosity and trust, and open a path for God.

PRAY

O come, o come, Emmanuel! God, come and dwell within me. Amen.

MONDAY, DECEMBER 10
SECOND WEEK OF ADVENT

BEGIN

"Be still, and know that I am God."

PRAY

Kindness and truth shall meet;
justice and peace shall kiss.
Truth shall spring out of the earth,
and justice shall look down from heaven.

~Psalm 85:10

LISTEN

Read Luke 5:17–26.

"Rise, pick up your stretcher, and go home."

~Luke 5:24

Jesus Comes to Set Us Free

Several years ago, the *New York Times* wrote about a man named Andrew Horton, who had died at age forty-three in a fire in a subway tunnel. What was most remarkable is that he had spent almost all his life living underground.

He had carved out a space in the dark where he was able to keep his things. But Andrew Horton wasn't just a vagabond. He was an artist and a writer. Tucked among his things, authorities found a manuscript for a graphic novel called *Pitch Black*. It described his life underground and some of his rules for living: "Always carry a light." "Anything you need can be found in the garbage." And "Always have a way out that is different from the way in."

That could be one of the lessons contained in this gospel passage. This is the story of man who met Jesus in an act of desperation and faith, but who was rewarded for his audacity. He was able to get up and walk out the front door, like anyone else, completely on his own.

His way out was different from his way in.

We all come to Christ with our own limitations, our own paralysis. Things that have left us crippled. It might not be a physical disease. It might be fear, dependency, or anger. So often, these emotions can leave us paralyzed, unable to move. We remain captives of our brokenness.

But the message of this gospel is one of liberation: Jesus sets us free. That sense of transforming hope is what compels us forward on our Advent journey— the assurance that God's entering our world changes everything.

No matter what is holding us back, no matter what keeps us from moving, he makes it possible for us to stand, rise, and walk.

ACT

Today, I will receive the sacrament of Penance and ask God for the grace to help me stand, rise, and walk.

PRAY

O come, o come, Emmanuel! God, free me from the chains of stubbornness, pride, and anger. Amen.

Tuesday, December 11
Second Week of Advent

BEGIN

"Be still, and know that I am God."

PRAY

Sing to the LORD a new song;
sing to the LORD, all you lands.
Sing to the LORD; bless his name;
announce his salvation, day after day.

~Psalm 96:1

LISTEN

Read Matthew 18:12–14.

"It is not the will of your heavenly Father that one of
these little ones be lost."

~Matthew 18:14

Awaiting a Shepherd

A couple years ago, I read a profile of a shepherd in Italy
named Fabrizio Innocenzi, who oversees about sixty
sheep in the hills of Roviano, a municipality forty miles
east of Rome.

Innocenzi said that sheep need a shepherd, because
they have no natural hierarchy, no leader of the flock.
The sheep learn to trust the shepherd, Innocenzi said,
as "they hear and understand the voice, the smell, the
behavior of the person who is looking after them every
day."

He said a shepherd needs to be someone who is "in
tune with nature, decisive" and willing to bear the long
hours, inclement weather, hard work, and sacrifice—and

do it out of devotion to his flock. A good shepherd, he said, should "not be afraid of anything." And as today's gospel indicates, he will do anything to keep the flock together, even searching for the lone sheep who has wandered away.

All this helps us to understand the point Jesus was making in this passage—and helps us to understand, as well, the overwhelming love that God has for each of us, the same love that would reveal itself so powerfully in the Incarnation. We should not lose sight of this beautiful reality during Advent: The great event of Christmas we are anticipating is more than a moment of angelic song. It is also a moment of sublime love. It is God saying, "I love you this much: I want to be one of you, to be with you, to reach out and rescue every one of you." How could any of us deny him that chance?

ACT

This day, I will offer a prayer of thanksgiving to God for loving me so much that he came into the world to live with me, search for me, find me, embrace me, and save me.

PRAY

O come, o come, Emmanuel! God, thank you for your love. Amen.

Wednesday, December 12
Feast of Our Lady of Guadalupe

BEGIN

"Be still and know that I am God."

PRAY

Your deed of hope will never be forgotten
by those who tell of the might of God.

~Judith 13:18

LISTEN

Read Luke 1:39–47.

"My soul proclaims the greatness of the Lord;
my spirit rejoices in God my savior."

~Luke 1:46–47

A Woman on a Journey

Soon a lot of us will be packing suitcases, piling into the minivan, or heading to the airport for the great Christmas travel nightmare. It's one of the busiest travel times of the year. So it seems fitting that this gospel today, right in the middle of our Advent journeying, reminds us of one of the great journeys and one of the great journeyers: Mary. In fact, it begins with her traveling—setting out in haste to visit her cousin, Elizabeth.

It's worth remembering that Mary was, throughout her life, a woman on a journey. She travels to Bethlehem, flees into Egypt, journeys to Jerusalem to find her lost son, and of course makes the long, heartbreaking trek to Calvary.

Mary remains for us a figure of tremendous tenacity, serenity, and trust—and one who never flinched from going wherever God would send her. I like to tell people she was not necessarily the fragile figure we see in porcelain statues. She was a woman of extraordinary strength and steadfast faith.

She is truly a model of discipleship—and, I think, a model of the first missionary. Even before Jesus was born, she was taking him into the world, bringing him to another, and proclaiming his greatness.

As we continue our own journeys through life—in particular, our Advent journey toward Christmas—may we be inspired by her determination, uplifted by her hope, and reassured by her unfailing tenderness and grace.

ACT

This time of year brings with it its own anxieties—maybe with family or friends, maybe with the pressures of holiday planning. Today, I will embrace Mary's example of serenity and remain calm when a family member, friend, or colleague adds to my already long to-do list.

PRAY

O come, o come, Emmanuel! God, help me see Mary as an example to guide me on my journey! Amen.

Thursday, December 13
Second Week of Advent

BEGIN

"Be still and know that I am God."

PRAY

I will extol you, my God and king;
I will bless your name forever and ever.

~*Psalm 145:1*

LISTEN

Read Matthew 11:11–15.

"Amen, I say to you,
among those born of women
there has been none greater than John the Baptist;
yet the least in the Kingdom of heaven is greater than
he."

~*Matthew 11:11*

Something—Someone—Is Coming

We tend to think of John the Baptist as the herald of the
Messiah, but in this gospel reading from Matthew, it
is the Messiah who heralds John the Baptist! "Among
those born of women," Jesus says, "there has been none
greater than John the Baptist." (Could anyone ask for a
better introduction than that?) There is a sense of both
expectation and mystery to what Jesus is saying. This
reading helps to underscore one of the great, recurring
themes of Advent: something—someone—is coming.
Yet there is a sense, too, of something drawing to a close.
Jesus speaks of violence, perhaps foreshadowing not
only John's brutal death, but also his own, and he tells

his followers to pay attention to what is happening and to what John is telling them.

"Whoever has ears," Jesus notes, "ought to hear." In other words, pay attention to the sign of the times. This is a stark and foreboding message for us to hear during this time of year. Shouldn't we be preparing for a star in the sky and a babe in a manger? Well, yes. But the challenge of this gospel is really the challenge of Advent—to make ourselves ready for Jesus to come into our world and into our hearts.

ACT

Remember to not lose sight of the sign of the times, even though celebrations have already begun. Today, offer a prayer for those impacted by current events such as wars, natural disasters, or gun violence.

PRAY

O come, o come, Emmanuel! Help me stand in solidarity with those who are weighed down by global events. Amen.

FRIDAY, DECEMBER 14
SECOND WEEK OF ADVENT

BEGIN

"Be still and know that I am God."

PRAY

For the LORD watches over the way of the just,
but the way of the wicked vanishes.

~Psalm 1:6

LISTEN

Read Matthew 11:16–19.

"Wisdom is vindicated by her works."

~Matthew 11:19

Nothing New under the Sun

Not long ago, a priest I know was ruminating about the early days of the Church and quoted one of his mother's favorite sayings, "There's nothing new under the sun." This saying could also apply to today's gospel passage. Throughout his earthly ministry, Jesus reminds his listeners just how fickle and petty human nature can be. He decries his generation as little more than spoiled children: pouting and judgmental, impatient and insufferable. And two thousand years later, nothing has changed.

From the very beginning, Christ knew that he could not alter human nature, but he came into the world to offer salvation and redemption to humanity, anyway. He comes to engage the human heart and bring about our conversion. This season of Advent, this season of expectation and waiting and hope, is also a time of transformation—a challenge to us all to effect change in our hearts and, by extension, begin, person by person and heart by heart, to change the world.

"This generation" Jesus addresses is really every generation. It is the generation of Pharisees, and the generation of Facebook followers who so quickly find fault and pick fights or pass judgment. There is nothing new under the sun and nothing new here being addressed by the Son. Jesus speaks to people of every age: all who are broken, wounded, prideful, or lost.

ACT

Today, when an annoyance arises, I will respond with patience.

PRAY

O come, o come, Emmanuel! Help me practice tolerance and choose joy today, and each day. Amen.

SATURDAY, DECEMBER 15
SECOND WEEK OF ADVENT

BEGIN

"Be still and know that I am God."

PRAY

Lord, make us turn to you; let us see your face and
we shall be saved.

~Psalm 80:2

LISTEN

Read Matthew 17:9a, 10–13.

"Elijah has already come, and they did not recognize
him but did to him whatever they pleased. So also
will the Son of Man suffer at their hands."

~Matthew 17:12

Be Prepared

Every Boy Scout knows these two simple words: be
prepared.

In fact, very often in life, we have to spend consid-
erable time and effort being prepared and *preparing*.
Whether it's painting a room, cooking a meal, or plant-
ing a garden, there is preparation involved. We may feel
this more acutely during these weeks before Christmas,
when so much planning and preparing has to go into the
holidays. Nothing of value just happens.

It's something we discover with these readings of
Advent—particularly when we encounter the Great
Preparer for the Messiah, John the Baptist. The gospel
today reminds us that Jesus didn't come into the world,
or into his ministry, without someone first making sure

the world was ready. John, in the passionate manner of Elijah, prepared the way.

These readings about John the Baptist also turn our hearts away from the merriment of December, toward something more somber: martyrdom. We remember that the forerunner of the Messiah suffered and died—just as the Messiah himself would.

In many ways, this can serve to deepen our experience of Advent. We realize just how great God's love is and how much was given for our salvation. And we recall, too, that courageous faith can all too often come with a high cost.

Advent is a season of anticipation and preparation, but we must also look beyond the festivities and the feasting. This is a good time to take stock and remember that, like the Boy Scouts, we need to be prepared.

ACT

Today I will offer a prayer of thanksgiving for those who prepared the way for my own faith journey, including parents, godparents, teachers, and mentors.

PRAY

O come, o come, Emmanuel! God, thank you for all Christians who have come before me and carried on the faith! Amen.

Sunday, December 16
Third Week of Advent

BEGIN

"Be still and know that I am God."

PRAY

The Spirit of the Lord is upon me,
because he has anointed me
to bring glad tidings to the poor.

~Isaiah 61:1

LISTEN

Read Luke 3:10–18.

Exhorting them in many other ways,
he preached good news to the people.

~Luke 3:18

What Is There Left for Us to Do?

Are you ready for Christmas?

Right around now, we start to hear that question a lot—and the answer is always "No!" There is never enough time. Christmas is only nine days away!

This particular Sunday, Gaudete Sunday, we turn our words and thoughts during Mass to rejoicing. But that feeling of joy is too often overwhelmed by a sense of panic. We check off a mental list: What is there left to do?

Well, people essentially asked John the Baptist that question in today's gospel and his answer was so simple: Be generous. Be fair. Be honorable. Give to those in need.

There's a story that's told of the Hebrew scholar Hillel, who lived a half a century before Christ. Some-one once asked him to sum up Jewish teaching in just a phrase, and he replied, "What is hateful to you, do not do to your fellow man. That is the whole of Torah. The rest is commentary. Now go and learn."

In this gospel, John the Baptist told his followers something similar. Generosity and fairness are not burdensome. They are rooted, first and foremost, in concern for others. Kindness is so basic and beautiful. And, it is all within our grasp.

That is something to rejoice over and to be grateful for.

As we begin the final days of Advent, we'll all be kept busy. There are wreaths to be hung, trees to be trimmed, lights to string. But John's words to his followers are a reminder: we should spend this time also doing some personal interior redecoration—taking a hard look at ourselves. We should be transforming not just our homes but also our hearts.

Look there. What is there left for us to do?

ACT

Today, I will look for opportunities to be more generous with my time, my talent, and my treasure. I will give of myself to those in need by offering to shop for an overwhelmed family member or donating change from purchases to charity.

PRAY

O come, o come, Emmanuel! God, you have given so much to me; help me imitate that generosity with others! Amen.

BEGIN

"Be still and know that I am God."

PRAY

May his name be blessed forever;
As long as the sun, his name shall remain.

~Psalm 72:17

LISTEN

Read Matthew 1:1–17.

The book of the genealogy of Jesus Christ,
the son of David, the son of Abraham.

~Matthew 1:1

Spiritual Roots

A couple of years ago, a colleague of mine at work received a DNA genealogy kit as a Christmas gift. He was fascinated and surprised to find that his background was not only Irish and Italian, as he expected, but also Russian and Eastern European. His family tree was a lot more complicated than he'd realized.

We might feel the same way when we hear the family tree, the genealogy of Jesus, in today's gospel. It is a long and exhaustive list of people and personalities, many of whom are obscure to most of us. But Matthew, in telling his account of the Good News, wanted to make clear that the protagonist had deep Jewish roots and so he begins with Abraham and concludes with Joseph and Mary, "of her was born Jesus who is called the Christ."

As we draw closer to Christmas, we cannot help but be moved to realize that all of human history, generation after generation after generation, has led to this moment when Christ came into the world. This beginning of Matthew's gospel is more than a laundry list of names; it is part of the story of our salvation history, history that we are a part of, history that we are about to celebrate again.

We might consider this account a kind of spiritual DNA genealogy kit, as it shows us where the roots of our faith begin. It offers us, at this moment in our Advent journey, an opportunity to pause and marvel at how the miracle of the Incarnation came to be.

A great old hymn invites us to "ponder anew / what the Almighty can do." What he can do with ordinary people in unlikely circumstances is indeed a wonder!

ACT

Sometimes I forget that Jesus, just like us, had deep roots, a family history that helped shape his earthly life. Today, I will say a prayer of thanksgiving for my own family—including those who are my extended family—remembering their strengths, weaknesses, and all they have given to me.

PRAY

O come, o come, Emmanuel! God, help me remember that family is a gift, not a burden. Amen.

Tuesday, December 18
Third Week of Advent

BEGIN

"Be still and know that I am God."

PRAY

Blessed be the Lord, the God of Israel,
who alone does wondrous deeds.
And blessed forever be his glorious name;
may the whole earth be filled with his glory.

~Psalm 72:18–19

LISTEN

Read Matthew 1:18–25.

"Behold, the virgin shall be with child and bear a son,
and they shall name him Emmanuel."

~Matthew 1:23

What Would Joseph Do?

At this late moment in our Advent journey, suddenly another member of the Holy Family steps into the spotlight. Joseph, a "righteous man" betrothed to Mary, is introduced. And given his moment, what does he do? He dreams. He listens to an angel. He trusts in the mercy and goodness of God.

Joseph, though one of the most familiar figures in the Christmas narrative, remains something of an enigma. We know little about him beyond his lineage and his livelihood. Mary utters one of the most beautiful prayers in all of scripture, the Magnificat; but Joseph never speaks a word. He is the silent member of the Holy Family—but his actions tell us all we need to know.

They speak eloquently of one man's ability to listen, to believe, to have courage, to take heart. They proclaim to the world the story of a faithful man giving credibility to the incredible, and boldly but quietly turning over his life and his future to something he can only take on faith.

Joseph has much to teach us, I think. How often do we doubt that God is on our side? How often do we wonder how our lives are supposed to unfold? How frequently do we find our plans upended by something we never expected—or could never even imagine? When this occurs, we should ask ourselves, what would Joseph do? This gospel's lesson: Look at what he did. Take heart. And do not be afraid.

ACT

During times of anxiety or doubt, I will trust in the words of an angel: do not be afraid. Joseph had faith that God would guide him. Today, when uncertainty arises, I will not succumb to anxiety but have faith in God's plans for my life.

PRAY

O come, o come, Emmanuel! God, help me trust in you, even when I cannot see the path ahead. Amen.

WEDNESDAY, DECEMBER 19
THIRD WEEK OF ADVENT

BEGIN

"Be still and know that I am God."

PRAY

For you are my hope, O LORD;
my trust, O God, from my youth.

~Psalm 71:17

LISTEN

Read Luke 1:5–25.

"You will have joy and gladness,
and many will rejoice at his birth,
for he will be great in the sight of the Lord."

~Luke 1:14

Can You Hear the Voice of God?

Bob Sheppard was one of the stars of the New York Yankees. He never threw a pitch or stole a base. But he was as much a part of Yankee Stadium as the wood in the bleachers and the smell of the popcorn and the roar of the crowd. Bob Sheppard was the stadium's announcer.

Everyone knew the game would not begin, could not begin, until they heard Bob Sheppard utter those immortal words: "Ladies and gentlemen, welcome to Yankee Stadium." When he died, some of his obituaries mentioned that Bob Sheppard was a devout Catholic, and went to Mass every day. He was also a lector at St. Christopher's, his parish on Long Island.

But to countless fans across generations, in Yankee Stadium, that great cathedral of baseball, Sheppard was known as "The Voice of God." When he spoke, people listened.

While we don't have "The Voice of God" in this gospel, we do have someone who speaks *for* him: the angel Gabriel. And it is a voice that announces extraordinary news—miracles and wonders that defy belief.

This passage is not just about news God wants us to hear but about whether we are willing and able to listen. Sometimes, to hear God we need to turn down the noise in the world around us. Other times, we ourselves need to be silent—which is exactly what happens to Zechariah.

Are we spending these days of preparation with our eyes, ears, and hearts open?

Advent is an opportunity for us to listen anew to the voice of God and, in a special way, to his messengers in the scripture and in our world.

ACT

What noise in my world or in my heart is drowning out God? Today I will seek moments of silence to listen deeply for the voice of God, meditating on his Word.

PRAY

O come, o come, Emmanuel! God, give me the grace to hear your voice! Amen.

Thursday, December 20
Third Week of Advent

BEGIN

"Be still and know that I am God."

PRAY

Who can ascend the mountain of the Lord?
or who may stand in his holy place?
He whose hands are sinless, whose heart is clean,
who desires not what is vain.

~Psalm 24:3–4

LISTEN

Read Luke 1:26–38.

Mary said, "Behold, I am the handmaid of the Lord.
May it be done to me according to your word."

~Luke 1:38

It Can Be Because God Wills It

Shortly before I was ordained, a teacher asked my class if anyone knew the one moment in scripture that was depicted in art more often than any other.

Everybody agreed, it must be the Nativity. But we were wrong. It's this moment we encounter in today's gospel: the Annunciation. Artists have painted it, sculpted it, and imagined it more than any other. It towers over the popular imagination.

You can speculate on the reasons why. It's certainly dramatic: This is the true beginning of the life of Christ, the very moment when our salvation began. And it is a perfect marriage of heaven and earth, the human and the divine.

But there is something else to it that I think speaks to us in a powerful way in the twenty-first century: the Annunciation is wildly, defiantly countercultural. It is a challenge that is offered—and, to our amazement, accepted.

Mary had the courage to listen to an angel. When Mary asked the question the world asks so often of God— "How can this be?"—the answer ignited in her a fire, the fire of possibility.

The answer is this: it can be because God wills it to be. Nothing is impossible with God.

Mary, we're told, was troubled at what she heard. But what follows is a message for all of us. In our moments when we are troubled by what God brings to us, know hope. Know trust. Know that light can break through the skies and guide the world to salvation in a stable.

At this dark moment in time, at this darkest time of the year, these final days of Advent, hope is proclaimed.

ACT

This gospel brings an unexpected visitor into Mary's world. How do I react to the Gabriels in my own life? Today I will seek to welcome the unexpected with an open heart, by treating strangers with the warmth I usually reserve for friends.

PRAY

O come, o come, Emmanuel! God, help me trust in your will for my life. Amen.

FRIDAY, DECEMBER 21
THIRD WEEK OF ADVENT

BEGIN

"Be still and know that I am God."

PRAY

Our soul waits for the LORD,
who is our help and our shield,
For in him our hearts rejoice;
in his holy name we trust.

~Psalm 33:20–21

LISTEN

Read Luke 1:39–45.

"Most blessed are you among women,
and blessed is the fruit of your womb."

~Luke 1:42

Embrace the Gift

A few years ago, I saw on the subway an ad for Cole Haan shoes that was a little out of the ordinary: there were no shoes and no pictures of people wearing shoes. There was just a phrase, printed on a dark background. It said: "No great story starts with: 'It was cold, so I stayed in . . .'"

I'm not sure what that has to do with shoes. But the tagline obviously made an impression. The implicit message: Take risks. Brave the weather. Great things can happen when you step out of your comfort zone.

Today's gospel is a vivid example of that. Mary leaves the comfort of her home in Nazareth, setting out into the rugged hills of Judah. And with that, a great heroic story begins—in fact, the greatest ever.

This is the story of Christianity—the ongoing and ever-new story of a gift being offered to the world.

This gospel passage is also, significantly, the particular story of Elizabeth: the saint of patience, the saint of eternal waiting, and the saint of Advent. In Luke's gospel, she is the first person mentioned, besides Mary, to encounter Christ. Think of it: before there were disciples and apostles, before the blind saw and the lame walked, there was Elizabeth. She was the first to welcome Jesus by welcoming his mother.

This gospel should fill us with Advent joy, as we get ready to welcome Jesus ourselves—and open our arms, like Elizabeth, to a miracle.

ACT

Mary took the courageous step of leaving her village and setting out alone to visit her cousin Elizabeth. What faith and trust! Today I will be more like Mary; I will call a family member or friend who has fallen out of touch.

PRAY

O come, o come, Emmanuel! God, help me bring faith and trust to all those I encounter! Amen.

Saturday, December 22
Third Week of Advent

BEGIN

"Be still and know that I am God."

PRAY

The LORD makes poor and makes rich,
he humbles, he also exalts.

~1 Samuel 2:4–5

LISTEN

Read Luke 1:46–56.

"My soul proclaims the greatness of the Lord."

~Luke 1:46

Mary, the Magnifier

I'm reaching the age when one of the most valuable tools we have around our house is a good magnifying glass. Need to read instructions? Directions on a pill bottle? The fine print on a warranty? The magnifying glass is our go-to.

Fulton Sheen once described Mary as "a magnifying glass that intensifies our love of her son." She helps us to see more clearly, understand more fully, and appreciate more deeply the transcendent reality of the Incarnation—and it all begins, really, with this prayer, her great proclamation we know as the Magnificat.

She speaks of how she cannot contain the wonder and greatness of God and needs to proclaim it to the world. What follows is a celebration of God's benevolent generosity and mercy—not just explained but magnified.

It comes moments after Elizabeth has greeted her; like any thoughtful guest, Mary has brought a gift for her cousin—this beautiful canticle—and it is a gift now shared with the world, generation after generation.

As Mary has magnified the Lord and proclaimed his greatness down through history, the question to us becomes: How do I? How do I express God's greatness to others, not just with my words but with my life—my actions, my choices, my giving of myself?

These weeks before Christmas are a time when we can be preoccupied with shopping for gifts. Perhaps one of the most valuable gifts we can offer is ourselves—living magnifying glasses helping, like Mary, to make the Lord brighter and clearer and more present in our world.

ACT

Mary proclaimed the greatness of the Lord. This day, I will remember God's generosity and share it with others, by donating to charity or buying a cup of coffee for a homeless person on the street.

PRAY

O come, o come, Emmanuel! God, I am grateful for all you have done for me! Amen.

SUNDAY, DECEMBER 23
FOURTH WEEK OF ADVENT

BEGIN

"Be still and know that I am God."

PRAY

O shepherd of Israel, hearken,
from your throne upon the cherubim, shine forth.
Rouse your power,
and come to save us.

~Psalm 80:2–3

LISTEN

Read Luke 1:39–45.

"And how does this happen to me,
that the mother of my Lord should come to me?"

~Luke 1:43

Carrying Christ

This could be one of the great, defining questions of Advent, when an astonished Elizabeth sees her young cousin at the door and realizes the source of humankind's salvation is about to enter her home.

"How does this happen to me?"

How does this gift happen to any of us? How are we so blessed as to receive God's grace in our lives? We can only wonder.

And wonder is the perfect sentiment for these last days of Advent. The Incarnation, God's becoming man, is the most wonder-filled act in human history. Soon enough, we will sing of it, and in the middle of a dark winter night, churches will be ablaze with light, overflowing with music and joy. But here, in this gospel passage, it is already beginning. And it is happening because of Mary—the visitor of the Visitation, the one who is full of grace.

Pope Benedict has called the Visitation the "first Eucharistic procession"—Mary, as living tabernacle, carries Christ to Elizabeth for adoration. But there is more. With this visit Mary taught us something so fundamental to our faith: *we need to bring Christ to others*. When Mary answered yes to the angel, she knew she had to share this, share *him*, with the world. That was her great vocation.

That, too, is ours. If you want to see the gospel mandate, here is where it begins. Here is our calling. Like Mary, we are called to bring Jesus in whatever way we can to a waiting world—to the lonely, the forgotten, the homebound, the neglected, the poor.

More than being just the "first Eucharistic procession," this moment also shows us the first moment of evangelization.

What a wonder! How does this happen to any of us?

ACT

During this day of prayerful preparation, I will share Christ with others, especially those like Elizabeth who may be elderly, shut-in, or alone.

PRAY

O come, o come, Emmanuel! God, through your Son, you have given me hope beyond measure. Amen.

Monday, December 24
Fourth Week of Advent

BEGIN

"Be still and know that I am God."

PRAY

O Radiant Dawn,
Splendor of eternal light, sun of justice:
come and shine on those who dwell in darkness and
in the shadow of death.

LISTEN

Read Luke 1:67–79.

"In the tender compassion of our God
the dawn from on high shall break upon us,
to shine on those who dwell in darkness and the
shadow of death,
and to guide our feet into the way of peace."

~Luke 1:78

Anticipating the Next Chapter

My most memorable Christmas Eve was the night I proposed to the woman who became my wife.

It sounds schmaltzy, and it was: we went out for a romantic dinner and, at desert, the waiter brought out a tray containing a small package: the engagement ring. (Spoiler alert: It was hardly a surprise. We'd been talking about getting married for months.) Everything after that was a blur, but I'll always think of that Christmas Eve as the best one of my life, when the most wondrous gift was delivered a day early.

This gospel, unfolding before us on Christmas Eve, offers another kind of wondrous gift on the day before the *greatest* gift: it's the Canticle of Zechariah, his beautiful prophecy about his son, who would become John the Baptist. It's one man's vision of a world about to be redeemed "in the tender compassion of our God." Here is a hope about to be realized, centuries of longing about to be fulfilled, millennia of expectation and waiting coming to a conclusion. A new moment in history is about to crack open.

For those of us completing this Advent journey, it is a moment to reflect and rejoice—and to feel renewed. The dawn will break. Light will beam. This evening, we may look around us with a sense of possibility and peace, to see garlands glimmering, candles burning, young faces scanning the horizon and trying to stay awake.

This sense of anticipation and hope is one we should savor in the last hours before we celebrate Christ's birth. The waiting is almost over.

But, as I remember thinking on that Christmas Eve so many years ago, the next great chapter is about to begin.

ACT

The last hours before Christmas can often be frenzied, stressful, sometimes full of pressure and panic. What did I forget to do? This day, I will let that go, for just a little while. I will take time not to worry about what I forgot but to *remember*—to remember what it has been about, to remember what the dawn will bring, to remember that the center of this celebration is the Prince of Peace.

PRAY

O come, o come, Emmanuel! God, you are with us! Amen.

TUESDAY, DECEMBER 25
THE NATIVITY OF THE LORD

BEGIN

"Be still and know that I am God."

PRAY

Let the heavens be glad and the earth rejoice;
let the sea and what fills it resound;
let the plains be joyful and all that is in them!
Then shall all the trees of the forest exult.

~Psalm 96:11–12

LISTEN

Read Luke 2:1–14.

"Behold, I proclaim to you good news of great joy
that will be for all the people.
For today in the city of David a savior has been born
for you who is Christ and Lord."

~Luke 2:10–11

Listen

A few years ago, I caught an episode of the cable TV
show *Inside the Actor's Studio*, hosted by James Lipton.
In this episode, he was interviewing Steven Spielberg.

Lipton asked Spielberg that final question that he
asks every guest on the program: "If you believe that
God exists, what do you hope he will say to you when
you finally see him?"

Spielberg thought for a moment and smiled. He
replied: "Thanks for listening."

So much of the Christmas story is truly about listening. It begins with Mary listening to an angel in

Nazareth. It is Elizabeth hearing Mary's voice—and John leaping within her. It is Joseph listening to his dreams. And in Luke's great retelling, we have shepherds listening with their flock outside Bethlehem, hearing for the first time the Good News.

This is the news that we have been waiting for, that all of creation has been listening for. God is with us! He has come into our lives and into our world.

Twenty centuries ago, shepherds listened and told the world what they heard, becoming the first missionaries. But God has no shepherds now but us. We are the ones chosen to hear his Good News—and to pass it on. It is news of wonder and hope.

It brings the sound of music filling the heavens, of hallelujahs in our hearts. This day, listen for it. Surrender to the joy. Carry it to others. And if we do, maybe one day we might hear God say, in gratitude and in joy, "Thanks for listening."

ACT

This day, I will open my heart to hear his quiet message of joy and hope through the noise of celebration and chaos of feasting; I will share his Good News with the world.

PRAY

O come, o come, Emmanuel! God, you are with us! Amen.

THE PSALMS OF CHRISTMAS

Next to the yearly celebration of the paschal mystery, the Church holds most sacred the memorial of Christ's birth and early manifestations. This is the purpose of the Christmas season. The Christmas season runs from Evening Prayer I of Christmas until the Sunday after Epiphany or after January 6, inclusive. The Mass of the Vigil of Christmas is used in the evening of December 24, either before or after Evening Prayer I. On Christmas itself, following an ancient tradition of Rome, three Masses may be celebrated: namely, the Mass at Midnight, the Mass at Dawn, and the Mass during the Day.

—General Norms for the Liturgical Year
and the Calendar, 32-34

On the following pages we offer you the Responsorial Psalms for the four Masses of Christmas. May they fill your Christmas season with boundless joy and deepest peace.

Christmas, Vigil Mass

Responsorial Psalm   Ps 89:4-5, 16-17, 27, 29

R. For ever I will sing the goodness of the Lord.
I have made a covenant with my chosen one,
    I have sworn to David my servant:
forever will I confirm your posterity
    and establish your throne for all generations.

R. For ever I will sing the goodness of the Lord.
Blessed the people who know the joyful shout;
    in the light of your countenance, O LORD, they
    walk.
At your name they rejoice all the day,
    and through your justice they are exalted.

R. For ever I will sing the goodness of the Lord.
He shall say of me, "You are my father,
    my God, the rock, my savior."
Forever I will maintain my kindness toward him,
    and my covenant with him stands firm.

R. For ever I will sing the goodness of the Lord.

Mass at Midnight

Responsorial Psalm   **Ps 96: 1-2, 2-3, 11-12, 13**

R. Today is born our Savior, Christ the Lord.
Sing to the LORD a new song;
     sing to the LORD, all you lands.
Sing to the LORD; bless his name.

R. Today is born our Savior, Christ the Lord.
Announce his salvation, day after day.
     Tell his glory among the nations;
     among all peoples, his wondrous deeds.

R. Today is born our Savior, Christ the Lord.
Let the heavens be glad and the earth rejoice;
     let the sea and what fills it resound;
     let the plains be joyful and all that is in them!
Then shall all the trees of the forest exult.

R. Today is born our Savior, Christ the Lord.
They shall exult before the LORD, for he comes;
     for he comes to rule the earth.
He shall rule the world with justice
     and the peoples with his constancy.

R. Today is born our Savior, Christ the Lord.

Mass at Dawn

Responsorial Psalm   Ps 97:1, 6, 11-12

R. A light will shine on us this day: the Lord is born for us.
The LORD is king; let the earth rejoice;
    let the many isles be glad.
The heavens proclaim his justice,
    and all peoples see his glory.

R. A light will shine on us this day: the Lord is born for us.
Light dawns for the just;
    and gladness, for the upright of heart.
Be glad in the LORD, you just,
    and give thanks to his holy name.

R. A light will shine on us this day: the Lord is born for us.

Mass during the Day

Responsorial Psalm   Ps 98:1, 2-3, 3-4, 5-6

R. All the ends of the earth have seen the saving power of God.
Sing to the LORD a new song,
>for he has done wondrous deeds;
his right hand has won victory for him,
>his holy arm.

R. All the ends of the earth have seen the saving power of God.
The LORD has made his salvation known:
>in the sight of the nations he has revealed his justice.
He has remembered his kindness and his faithfulness
>toward the house of Israel.

R. All the ends of the earth have seen the saving power of God.
All the ends of the earth have seen
>the salvation by our God.
Sing joyfully to the LORD, all you lands;
>break into song; sing praise.

R. All the ends of the earth have seen the saving power of God.
Sing praise to the LORD with the harp,
>with the harp and melodious song.
With trumpets and the sound of the horn
>sing joyfully before the King, the LORD.

R. All the ends of the earth have seen the saving power of God.

Greg Kandra serves as a deacon in the Diocese of Brooklyn, is a multimedia editor at the Catholic Near East Welfare Association, and is the author of *The Deacon's Bench* blog on Patheos. He was a writer and producer for CBS News from 1982 to 2008 for programs including *The CBS Evening News with Katie Couric*, *Sunday Morning*, *60 Minutes II*, and *48 Hours*. Kandra also served for four years as a writer and producer on the live finale of the hit reality show *Survivor*.

Kandra has received two Peabody and two Emmy awards, four Writers Guild of America awards, three Catholic Press Association Awards, and a Christopher Award for his work. He also was named 2017 Clergy of the Year by the Catholic Guild of Our Lady of the Skies Chapel at JFK International Airport. He earned a bachelor's degree in English from the University of Maryland. Kandra cowrote the acclaimed CBS documentary *9/11*. He contributed to three books, including Dan Rather's *Deadlines and Datelines*, and a homily series. His work has been published in *America*, *US Catholic*, *Busted Halo*, and *The Brooklyn Tablet*. He has been a regular guest on Catholic radio, including Gary Zimak's *Spirit in the Morning* and is a regular contributor to *Give Us This Day*.

Kandra lives with his wife, Siobhain, in the New York City area.